TAFSEER SURAH FATIHAH & CLARIFYING THE CATEGORIES OF TAWHEED IN IT

BY SHAYKH HAMMAAD IBN MUHAMMAD AL-ANSAAREE

ISBN: 978-1-4675-7769-4

First Edition: Sha'ban 1434 A.H. / June 2013 C.E.

Cover Design: Maktabatulirshad staff

E-mail: Maktabatulirshad@gmail.com

Typesetting and Editing: Aboo Sulaymaan Muhammad 'Abdul-Azim bin Joshua Baker

Subject: Tafseer

Website: www.maktabatulirshad.webs.com

E-mail: Maktabatulirshad@gmail.com

فِهْرِس

TABLE OF CONTENTS

BIOGRAPHY OF AUTHOR

Shaykh Hammaad ibn Muhammad al-Ansaaree:

He was Abu 'Abdul-Lateef Hammaad ibn Muhammad ibn Muhammad ibn Hinnah ibn Mukhtaar ibn Muhammad al-Basheer, from the lineage of Qays ibn Sa'd ibn 'Ubaadah al-Khazrajee al-Ansaaree, who was born in 1343 A.H. (1924 C.E.) in a town called Taad Makkah in Mali, West Africa. The name Taad Makkah means "this is Makkah" since it is surrounded by 4 mountains as Makkah itself is. His family was well known in Timbuktu which was the capital of the eastern region of Mali. His lineage ends at Banee Naseer al-Ansaariyyeen who were the last to rule Gharnaatah (Granada, Andalus (Spain)). His family was known for their knowledge, giving fataawa and adjudication before and after the French colonized Mali.

His upbringing and seeking knowledge and his Shuyookh

The Shaykh was brought up in a house of excellence and knowledge, since his Shaykhs were:

1) His paternal uncle, Shaykh al-Muqri. Muhammad ibn Ahmad ibn Taqqee al-Ansaaree, who was nicknamed "Teacher of Children" for the time he spent devoted to them and teaching them to recite the Quraan. So Shaykh Hammaad began by memorizing the Quraan when he was

ten years old until he completed memorizing it and reciting it with tajweed as the age of 15 years. He also studied nahoo and sarf under the tutelage of his uncle;

2) His paternal uncle's son, the 'Allaamah of his time - Shaykh Moosaa ibn al-Kisaa.ee Al-Ansaaree;

3) His maternal uncle, Muhammad ibn Ahmad ibn Muhammad, who was nicknamed "al-Bahr" (the sea) for the immense knowledge which he had. Shaykh Hammaad studied usool al-fiqh and tafseer under his tutelage as he also studied Imaam Maalik's ((al-Muwattaa.)) And the Saheeh of both Imaam al-Bukhaaree and Imaam Muslim, as well as the Sunan of Abu Daawood, amongst other works such as ((Mukhtasir Khaleel)) and books of the Maalikee fiqh;

4) Shaykh ash-Shareef al-Idreesee al-Husaynee Hamood ibn Muhammad, under whose tutelage he studied philosophy, usool al-fiqh and tafseer.

Thereafter Shaykh Hammaad continued studying the major books and also began teaching in the town of Manaaqah until he made hijrah after the French colonization of Mali.

So when Shaykh Hammaad reached Makkah, he joined the study circles of the 'ulamaa. Amongst who was:

1) Shaykh Muhammad 'Abdur-Razzaaq Hamzah who used to teach ((Tafseer Ibn Katheer));

2) Shaykh Abu Muhammad 'Abdul-Haqq al-'Amree al-Haashimee al-Hindee, who used to teach the Saheeh of Imaam al-Bukhaaree;

3) Shaykh Hasan al-Mashaat, who used to teach ((Sunan at-Tirmidhee));

4) Shaykh Muhammad Ameen al-Hanafee, who used to teach the Saheeh of Imaam al-Bukhaaree;

5) Shaykh al-'Arabee at-Tabaanee;

6) Shaykh Muhammad Ameen al-Halabee, who used to teach nahoo;

7) Shaykh Haamid al-Fiqhee;

...And other than them from the scholars of al-Masjid al-Haraam in Makkah.

His journey to Madeenah

Shaykh Hammaad travelled to Madeenah, where he studied in the Daar al-'Uloom ash-Shar'iyyah in 1371 A.H. (1952 C.E.), in the faculty specializing in hadeeth. Whilst in Madeenah, he studied under many of its shuyookh, amongst them:

1) Shaykh Muhammad 'Abdullaah ibn Mahmood al-Madanee, who was the imaam of al-Masjid

an-Nabawee. Shaykh Hammaad benefitted tremendously from Shaykh al-Madanee that he wrote a book about him;

2) Shaykh Muhammad ibn Turkee an-Najdee, under whose tutelage he studied Imaam Maalik's ((al-Muwattaa.)) And Ibn Qudaamah's ((al-Mughnee));

3) Shaykh Muhammad al-Haafidth ibn Moosaa Hameed under whose tutelage he studied ((Sunan an-Nasaa.ee)), And thereupon he was granted an ijaazah (permission to teach it);

4) Shaykh 'Umar Baree;

5) Shaykh 'Ammaar al-Maghrabee;

6) Shaykh 'Abdul Khuday'.

His return to Makkah

After Shaykh Hammaad graduated from Daar al-'Uloom ash-Shar'iyyah in 1371 A.H. (1952 C.E.) he returned to Makkah where he worked as a teacher in accordance with what his paternal uncle's son - Shaykh Ismaa'eel al-Ansaaree - had written to him since he too was working as a teacher there in Makkah.

So Shaykh Hammaad returned to Makkah to teach in the first year of a primary school and the second year of a secondary school, and the third and fourth year of higher studies. Here, he met up with Shaykh 'Abdul-Lateef ibn Ibraaheem Aal ash-Shaykh and his brother Shaykh Muhammad ibn Ibraaheem Aal ash-Shaykh. Upon visiting them, he found them in the company of their brother Shaykh 'Abdul-Malik ibn Ibraaheem Aal ash-Shaykh to whom he was introduced.

Later, Shaykh 'Abdul-Lateef suggested to Shaykh Hammaad that he go to Riyadh, whereupon he ordered his secretary to call 'Abdul-'Azeez al-Lajaawee who was responsible for the teaching staff of all the universities.

In accordance with Shaykh 'Abdul-Lateef's request, Shaykh Hammaad performed Hajj and then departed for Riyadh, where he began teaching in the Faculty of Sharee'ah. Shaykh Hammaad also taught at the Institute of Imaam ad-Da'wah in Riyadh, which was setup at that time, and where he remained from 1375 A.H. (1956 C.E.) until 1378 A.H. (1959 C.E.). He then returned to the Faculty of Sharee'ah where he remained from 1379 A.H. (1960 C.E.) until 1384 A.H (1965 C.E.).

In 1384, A.H., (1965 C.E.) he travelled to Madeenah where he transferred to the Islaamic University until he retired in 1410 A.H. (1991 C.E.). However, he remained in touch with the Islaamic University, where he supervised Masters and Doctorate students preparing their theses.

The Shuyookh who granted him an ijaazah

1) Shaykh 'Ubaydur-Rahmaan al-Mubaarakphooree, who was the author of ((Mir'aatul-Mafaateeh Sharh Mishkaatul-Masaabeeh));

2) Shaykh 'Abdul-Hafeedth al-Filisteenee;

3) Shaykh Qaasim ibn 'Abdul-Jabbaar al-Andeejaanee;

4) Shaykh Hamood at-Tuwayjaree;

5) Shaykh Abu Muhammad 'Abdul-Haqq al-Haashimee.

His travels

Shaykh Hammaad had a strong desire to travel to a number of countries, which he did, such that he was known to say: ((I endeavor to travel the world over, even to China, however, my age has not permitted me to do so)). From the countries to which he travelled were: Egypt, Syria, Morocco, India and other than them from the European, African and Asian countries. The Shaykh has recorded his travels in his book ((ar-Rihlaat al-Ansaariyyah)).

His teachings

In addition to his teaching commitments at the Islaamic University, Shaykh Hammaad was very conscientious in teaching the books of the Sunnah and Tawheed. Amongst the books he taught were:

((Saheeh Muslim)), ((Saheeh al-Bukhaaree)), ((Sunan at-Tirmidhee)) - which he taught in al-Masjid an-Nabawee, ((at-Tawheed wa Ithbaat Sifaat ar-Rabb)) of Imaam Ibn Khuzaymah, ((Sharh al-'Aqeedah at-Tahaawiyyah)) and other than these books.

His participation in gatherings of knowledge

Shaykh Hammaad was a member of the committee of the Centre for Research into the Sunnah and Seearah of the Prophet in Madeenah. He was also a member of the supervisory committee for administration affairs of al-Masjid an-Nabawee, which met twice a week.

His library

Shaykh Hammaad started his library in 1367 A.H. (1948 C.E.), and in the beginning it contained books covering all aspects of knowledge. Later in 1373 A.H. (1954 C.E.) he gifted his library to his paternal uncle, and thereafter began to build up his library from new, only this time concentrating on the area of hadeeth.

His library grew daily, containing books on hadeeth, 'ilm ar-rijaal (science of the narrators of hadeeth), mustalah (science of hadeeth terminology) and all other aspects of hadeeth and 'aqeedah, in addition to research papers from, the Islaamic University and other universities within Saudi Arabia. Indeed, in building up his vast collection of books, the Shaykh spared no expense in collecting those books which interested him.

He bought the book ((Taareekh Damishq)) of Ibn 'Asaakir which in itself, cost the Shaykh seven thousand riyals (approximately £1,200 / $2,000). Likewise, the book ((al-Kaamil)) of Ibn 'Adee which he brought over from Turkey, cost him one thousand riyals (approximately £180 / $300), and this was at a time when his salary was only a mere one thousand riyals.

The Shaykh kindly kept his library open in the morning and early evening for students of knowledge and researchers alike, such that after his death, his children agreed to take on the responsibility of running his library and keeping it open to students of knowledge and researchers, just as their father had done when he was alive. May Allaah reward Shaykh Hammaad for the benefit being sought from his vast library, and his children for maintaining it, Aameen.

Shaykh Hammaad was devoted to collecting books, in particular books on hadeeth and 'Aqeedah. So whenever a new book was printed he was amongst the first to get hold of a copy, whether it be in Madeenah or outside Madeenah. And if he heard a new book has been published he will call the publisher or distributor of that particular book and ask them to send him a copy for his ever-growing library.

His knowledge of books was so vast; it was as if he was a walking point of reference. So whenever students used to visit him, many a time they would begin by asking him about any new publications or whether he had bought any new manuscripts.

His poetry

Shaykh Hammaad was well known for his mastery of writing poetry.

The Shuyookh's praise of him

Many of the Shuyookh bore witness to his vast knowledge, amongst them were:

1) Shaykh 'Abdul-'Azeez ibn Baaz;

2) Shaykh Muhammad Naasiruddeen al-Albaanee;

3) Shaykh 'Abdul-'Azeez ibn 'Abdullaah Aal ash-Shaykh - currently the muftee of Saudi Arabia;

4) Shaykh Saalih ibn Muhammad al-Luhaydaan
- head of the senior council of judges in Saudi
Arabia;

5) Shaykh 'Abdul-Muhsin ibn Hamad al-'Abbaad
- previously the deputy president of the Islaamic
University of Madeenah

...And other than them from the scholars of the
Islaamic world.

His students

Shaykh Hammaad had many students, amongst
those to whom he granted an ijaazah were:

1) 'Attiyah Muhammad Saalim - who studied
((al-Aajaro Miyah)) and ((ar-Rahabiyyah)) under
him;

2) Shaykh Dr. Saalih ibn Sa'd as-Suhaymee;

3) Shaykh Dr. Marzooq ibn Hiyaas az-
Zahraanee;

4) Shaykh Dr. 'Umar ibn Hasan Fallaatah;

5) Shaykh Dr. Baasim Faysal al-Jawaabirah;

6) Shaykh Dr. Wasee-ullaah 'Abbaas;

7) Shaykh Dr. 'Abdul-'Aleem 'Abdul-'Atheem;

8) Shaykh Dr. Mahfooth ar-Rahmaan Zayn;

9) Shaykh Dr. Falaah ibn Ismaa'eel;

10) Shaykh Dr. Falaah ibn Thaanee as-Sa'eedee

...And other than them from his students.

His house

Shaykh Hammaad used to live in Haarah al-Masaani', in Madeenah, and at that time his house was overflowing with students of knowledge and researchers. Later, he had a larger house built in Haarah ash-Sharqiyyah. Sometime later, his library outgrew this house, and Prince Sultan ibn 'Abdul-'Azeez gifted him a much bigger house in Hayy al-Faysaliyyah next to the Islaamic University. The Shaykh remained in this house, as in the previous houses, upon the same pattern of opening the doors of his library to those who wished to seek benefit from his vast collection of books.

His illness and death

Shaykh Hammaad became ill on the night of 23 Ramadhaan in 1417 A.H. (1998 C.E.) whilst performing his night prayers in al-Masjid an-Nabawee. His illness became severe and he died on the morning of Wednesday 21 Jumaada Awwal 1418 A.H. after spending nearly eight months in hospital.

His funeral prayer was performed after Salaatul-
'Asr in al-Masjid an-Nabawee, and he was then
buried in the graveyard of Baqee'. Indeed the
masses who turned out for his funeral was a
sight; It caused one to remember the saying of
Imaam Ahmad who said: ((**Say to the people of
innovation (ahlul-bid'ah): Between you and us
are the funerals**)), implying the great numbers
who attend the funerals of Ahlus-Sunnah and
the few who attend the funerals of Ahlul-Bid'ah.

Many attended his funeral from amongst the
scholars and the judges and lecturers and
teachers from the universities along with many
students.

His children

Shaykh Hammaad died leaving one wife and
eleven children; Amongst them eight sons,
including 'Abdul-Baaree and 'Abdul-Awwal who
both graduated from the Faculty of Hadeeth
(Islaamic University of Madeenah). 'Abdul-
Baaree also attained a Masters and now teaches
in the Faculty of Hadeeth. As for 'Abdul-Awwal,
he works as a researcher in the Centre for
Research into the Sunnah and Seearah of the
Prophet in Madeenah. Shaykh Hammaad also
left behind 3 daughters. May Allaah
(Subhaanahu wa Ta'aala) have Mercy upon his
soul, aameen.

INTRODUCTION

In the name of Allaah, All praise is due to Allaah Lord of all that exist and peace and forgiveness be upon the noblest of prophets and messengers, our prophet Muhammad, his family, all of his companions, and those who follow them perfectly until the Day of Judgment.

As for what follows;

Indeed the most truthful of speech is the book of Allaah, and the best guidance is the guidance of Muhammad (peace and blessings be upon him and his family). The evilest of affairs are novelties, and every novelty is innovation, every innovation is misguidance, and every misguidance is in the hellfire. Whatever Allaah wills, and there is neither trying nor power except with Allaah. I seek refuge with Allah from the cursed satin,

بِسْمِ ٱللَّهِ ٱلرَّحْمَٰنِ ٱلرَّحِيمِ ۝ ٱلْحَمْدُ لِلَّهِ رَبِّ ٱلْعَٰلَمِينَ ۝ ٱلرَّحْمَٰنِ ٱلرَّحِيمِ ۝ مَٰلِكِ يَوْمِ ٱلدِّينِ ۝ إِيَّاكَ نَعْبُدُ وَإِيَّاكَ نَسْتَعِينُ ۝ ٱهْدِنَا ٱلصِّرَٰطَ ٱلْمُسْتَقِيمَ ۝ صِرَٰطَ ٱلَّذِينَ أَنْعَمْتَ عَلَيْهِمْ غَيْرِ ٱلْمَغْضُوبِ عَلَيْهِمْ وَلَا ٱلضَّآلِّينَ ۝

With the name Allaah the most Merciful and Gracious. All praise is due to Allaah Lord of all that exist. Owner of the Day of Judgment. You alone we worship, and You alone we seek aid. (We beg you to) guide us the straight path. The path of those whom You have

bestowed Your bounty upon them, not the path of those who have a wrath upon them nor those who are astray.[1] *Ameen.*

This tremendous chapter is recommended for every Muslim to know generally some of the noble meanings that only a few has brought attention to that is included in it. We know this chapter is recited every day by every Muslim in all prayers whether it be obligatory prayers or voluntary prayers, and if the reader reflect over the hidden secrets and wisdom of it, truly he would be diligently trying to understand it and to know what the hidden secrets are in this chapter that is repeatedly recited in every prayer. Which something that is not found in any other chapters of the Quran whether they be long, medium, or short chapters.

For this reason, I saw fit to give as a gift to the brothers some of what Allaah has granted me of success from this chapter of those meanings that which if anyone was granted the success of being able to explain and clarify it then it is something that requires a long period of time doing so. However, we say that which all of it cannot be reached does not mean all of it should be left.

We say with Allaah we seek assistance

ဢ ✸ ✸ ✸ ၶ

---

[1] Fatihah [1:1-7]

BOOKS ON AL-FATIHAH

This is chapter, (Al-Fatihah) because of its tremendous importance, virtue, and nobility books have been written about it alone like Shaykhul Islam Ibn Taymiyyah wrote a separate individual treatise about it that is highly beneficial. [2]

When you read the existing explanations (for Al-Fatihah) that exist, you find that Shaykhul Islam has condensed all of those explanations most important matters in his treatise.

At the forefront of those explanations is "Tafseer At-Tabari" which is the greatest in existence today because of its distinguished characteristics that do not exist in any other explanation that has been found or heard of. Anyone who has read this (Tafseer At-Tabari) explanation scrutinizing it with precision would arrive at this conclusion.

Also, the student of Shaykhul Islam رحمه الله (mercy of Allaah be upon him) Ibn Qayyim isolated this chapter for explanation within his well-known book "*Madarijul Salikeen Sharhu Manazilis Sa'ireen Lil-Harawi*". This explanation was taken and isolated in this book as an independent explanation for Al-Fatihah. [3]

---

2 Majmoo' Fatawa [14v:4-40]

3 among those who isolated Al-Fatihah for explanation based from the book "Madarij" and others, author of the book "Badai'u At-Tafseer" [vol.1;107-257]

DIFFERENT NAMES FOR AL-FATIHAH

This magnificent chapter has many names, and many names indicate the nobility of the appellation. From its names are:

1. **Al-Fatihah (The Opening)**. It is called this because the prayer opens with it in the beginning and for other reasons.

2. **The Magnificent Quran**

3. **The Seven Most Repeated** [4]

4. **The Healer**

5. **The Sufficient**. [5]

The meaning of it being "the sufficient" because it is sufficient and independent of anything else while other things are not sufficient from it, if you recite the whole Quran from Baqarah in one unit of prayer from the units of prayer until the chapter of Naas then you prayer would not be

---

[4] footnote: for the hadeeth Abi Sa'eed Ibn Al mu'alaa collected by Bukhaari (hadeeth #4474) in it the Prophet's (peace be upon him) statement **"It is the seven most repeated and the Magnificent Quran"** and for the hadeeth of Abi Hurairah raised to the Prophet (peace be upon him): **"Mother of the Quran is the Seven Most Repeated and the Magnificent Quran"** Bukhari collected it (hadeeth #3704)

[5] Look in Fathu alBaari (vol. 8; 156) and Adurrul Maatur (vol. 1; 10-15)

correct, rather it would be null and void. At the same time if you limit or shorten the whole prayer with reciting Al-Fatihah truly the prayer would be accepted. This is the meaning of it being "the sufficient".

Every one of its meanings indicates a noble meaning and a noble meaning prove the high status of this tremendous chapter.

SURAH AL-FATIHAH WAS REVEALED WHERE?

The scholars of tafseer differ in regards to which place this Surah was revealed; was it revealed in Mecca or Madinah?

There are narrated statements, but all of them are unauthentic except one statement, and that is that it was revealed in the noble city of Mecca.

What makes this statement the authentic acceptable one is that which comes in the Book of Allaah of clear proof proving this Surah was revealed in Mecca is his statement the Most High,

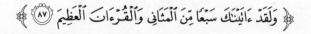

"Truly We have given you the seventh most recited verses (Saba'a Al-Mathaani) and a Magnificent Quran". 6

This verse is from Surah al Hijr, and it is Meccan. And from there all other statements that others have narrated, narrated them with chains that are flimsy, shabby, and weak therefore, deemed as unauthentic statements not to be relied upon. This is because some of them say: *"It was revealed in Medina"* others have said *"It was revealed twice, once in Medina and once in Mecca"* statements like this. So the

---

6 Al-Hijr [15:87]

correct statement is the first statement mentioned in the verse from Suratul-Hijr. The two meanings of *Mathaani* are in this verse from Suratul-Hijr.

The 1st meaning: It is called *Mathaani* because it is repeated in every prayer whereas if it is not recited in every unit of prayer whether obligatory or optional prayers that prayer is truly invalid. Just as the hadeeth (narration) comes:

مَنْ لَمْ يَقْرَأْ بِفَاتِحَةِ الْكِتَابِ فَصَلَاتُهُ خِدَاجٌ .

"Whoever does not recite the opening of the Book, then his prayer is Khidaaj" [7]

Meaning: *"it is deficient, incomplete"*

The 2nd meaning: that it is inclusive to Allaah being praised in a manner that no other chapter in the Quran includes. However the first meaning is proven by many texts, even though the second meaning is also correct. As for it being seven verses, the scholars differ upon that. Some of them say, *"it is seven verses with basmalah (the verse bismillahirRahmaanirRaheem)."* Others say, *"basmallah is not from the Quran or it is not from Al-Fatihah."*

Among those Qudsi narrations that have come about its virtue is: on the authority of Abu

---

Hurairah (ﷺ) (may Allaah be pleased with him) said: "I heard the Messenger of Allaah ﷺ (forgiveness and safety of Allah be upon him and his family) saying "Allaah –the mighty and sublime-said:

قَسَمْتُ الصَّلَاةَ بَيْنِي وَ بَيْنَ عَبْدِي نِصْفَيْنِ : فَإِذَا قَالَ : ﴿ ٱلْحَمْدُ لِلَّهِ رَبِّ ٱلْعَٰلَمِينَ ﴾ ، قَالَ اللهُ عَزَّ وَ جَلَّ : حَمِدَنِي عَبْدِي ، فَإِذَا قَالَ الْعَبْدُ : ﴿ ٱلرَّحْمَٰنِ ٱلرَّحِيمِ ﴾ ، قَالَ اللهُ عَزَّ وَ جَلَّ : أَثْنَى عَلَيَّ عَبْدِي ، وَ إِذَا قَالَ الْعَبْدُ : ﴿ مَٰلِكِ يَوْمِ ٱلدِّينِ ۝٤ ﴾ ، قَالَ اللهُ عَزَّ وَ جَلَّ : مَجَّدَنِي عَبْدِي ، وَ إِذَا قَالَ الْعَبْدُ : ﴿ إِيَّاكَ نَعْبُدُ وَإِيَّاكَ نَسْتَعِينُ ۝٥ ﴾ ، قَالَ اللهُ عَزَّ وَ جَلَّ : هَذَا بَيْنِي وَ بَيْنَ عَبْدِي ، وَ لِعَبْدِي مَا سَأَلَ ، وَ إِذَا قَالَ الْعَبْدُ : ﴿ ٱهْدِنَا ٱلصِّرَٰطَ ٱلْمُسْتَقِيمَ ﴾ ﴿ صِرَٰطَ ٱلَّذِينَ أَنْعَمْتَ عَلَيْهِمْ غَيْرِ ٱلْمَغْضُوبِ عَلَيْهِمْ وَلَا ٱلضَّآلِّينَ ﴾ ، قَالَ اللهُ عَزَّ وَ جَلَّ : هَذَا لِعَبْدِي ، وَ لِعَبْدِي مَا سَأَلَ .

"I have split the prayer between me and my servant in two halves," when he says: "AlhamdulillahirabbiAalamin." Allaah says: "My slave has praised me". And when he says: "ArRahmaanirRaheem." Allaah says:

"My servant has applauded me" and when he says: "maalikiyawmideen" Allaah says: "My servant has glorified me". When he (the servant) says: "iyyaaka na'budu wa iyyaaka nasta'een", Allaah says: "This is between me and my servant and for my servant is what he asks for". When he says: "ihdinassiratal mustaqeem, siraatalladheena an'amta alaihim. Ghairil maghdubi alahim waladhaalleen" Allaah says: "This is for my servant and for my servant is what he asks for".

Malik collected this hadeeth in his "Muwatta" in the chapter "Characteristics of Prayer".[8] Al-Fatihah is called prayer (Salah) because the prayer is not correct except with reciting it just as the narration states,

مَنْ لَمْ يَقْرَأْ بِفَاتِحَةِ الْكِتَابِ فَصَلَاتُهُ خِدَاجٌ .

"Whoever does not recite the opening of the Book, then his prayer is Khidaaj"

Meaning: *"it is deficient, incomplete.* [9]

൭ ✿ ✿ ✿ ൠ

---

[8] Al-Muwatta: Book of prayer: chapter reciting behind the Imaam when there isn't out loud reciting (vol. 1/ 84-85). And Muslim collected it in his authentic: Book of Prayer; Chapter: Obligation of Reciting Al-Fatihah (vol. 1/ 296 and 395).
[9] Muwatta: The Book of Prayer, Muslim: Book of Prayer.

A CLARIFICATION THAT SURATUL-FATIHAH IS ONE OF THOSE CHAPTERS SPECIFIED FOR TAWHEED

This Surah is a sum of chapters that have been isolated for Tawheed and they are four chapters of the Noble Quran: Al-Fatihah, Al- Kaafirun, Al-Ikhlaas, and Al-Falaq. Each one of them arranges and organizes the aspects of Tawheed that is specified for it.

For example, Suratul-Fatihah collects all categories of Tawheed, whereas Al-Kafirun includes Tawheed Al Uloohiyyah (unity in Allaah's worship); Ikhlaas contains Tawheed Al Asmaa was-sifaat (unity in Allaah's names and attributes), and Suratul Falaq contains Tawheed Ar-ruboobiyyah (Unity in Allaah's lordship).

If this indicates anything, it truly indicates the importance of Tawheed because Allaah is the one who revealed Tawheed and each of its categories all in one complete Surah that which does not exist in regards to fiqh or subsidiary issues at all. Just as Allaah says:

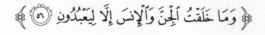

$$﴾ وَمَا خَلَقْتُ ٱلْجِنَّ وَٱلْإِنسَ إِلَّا لِيَعْبُدُونِ ۝ ﴿$$

"I have not created jinkind or mankind but to worship me". [10]

---

[10] Dhariyaat [51:56]

His statement "to worship me" is Tawheed. The first command encountered in the Book of Allaah is the commandment of worship as in Suratul-Baqarah,

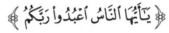

"O mankind worship your lord" [11]

Therefore, we realize that these four chapters of the Quran were revealed to us inclusive to Tawheed; and all that point towards the importance of Tawheed, which is the hidden secret behind the creation of jinkind and mankind. Why is Suratul-Fatihah at the forefront of all the other chapters of the Quran? Why? Because this Surah contains the whole message of the Quran in it, there is not a verse in the Quran except what it contains already exists in this Surah, and one who realize this know it and whoever is ignorant of this is ignorant. That is the case because this Surah has three main components that make up the whole Quran:

1. **Tawheed:** which is the foundation
2. **Targheeb:** (encouraging) or **Wa'd** (promises)
3. **Tarheeb:** (frightening) or **Wa'eed** (threats). These last two are branches of the foundation.

---

[11] Al-Baqarah [2-21]

It has these three affairs along with what will be mentioned afterwards of what people have published based on these three matters.

Gathering between Targheeb and Tarheeb or making desirable obedience and making fearful disobedience after it explains to us Tawheed is a custom of Allaah that flows all through His Wise Book. Since Allaah mentions all of the categories of Tawheed and follows that up with encouraging to Tawheed and warning against what opposes it, then people will publish books on based on their acting out Tawheed and their connection to it.

When we read the Quran from beginning of Baqarah to the end of Naas, we would not find one verse except with these three matters is abstracted from them.

What is suitable for us to mention now in relation to this chapter including these three matters is the statement: *"Your limiting this Surah or all of the Quran to just these three matters, how can it compare to the statement of some scholars who say: "Truly the Quran contains more than these three matters juts as the poet says":*

حَلَالٌ ، حَرَامٌ، مُحْكَمٌ، مُتَشَابِهٌ

بَشِيرٌ، نَذِيرٌ، قِصَّةٌ، عِظَةٌ، مَثَلْ

"The Quran consists of permissible, prohibited, clear, and ambiguous, bringer of good, Warner of evil, stories, admonition, and examples" [12]

Like this some of the people of knowledge say:

"Indeed the whole Quran research about these affairs that are included in this poem, and in your (the author) words you limit the Quran to just these three things that are only a third of those nine there still remains two-thirds. So how can success be found in what this poem contains and what you presented?"

Answer: These nine matters this poem contains all of it return to the three I mentioned. This aspect comes to light when you said, *"permissible and prohibited"*, **"permissible"** is the promise, and **"prohibited"** is the threat. Likewise, the words **Muh'kam** (clear verses) and **Mutashabih** (ambiguous verses) also enters into the promise of Allaah and the threat of Allaah.

As for the meaning of **Muh'kam** "clear verses" they are verses that only accept one meaning. **Mutashabih** "Ambiguous verses" are verses that carry numerous meanings, some are correct, and some are incorrect. These types of verses also fall into **"the promise"** and **"the threat"** of Allaah because verses that fall into "promise of

---

[12] Look in the book: *"Ruhul-Almaani"* (vol. 8/127)

Allaah" are either "clear" or "ambiguous" and we
already know the meaning of them both.

So **Muh'kam** is an expression for every verse in
the Quran that only carries one meaning. Like
his statement The Most High,

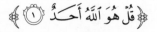

"Say: He Allah is one"

Therefore, this verse only has one meaning that
it could carry. The verse is informing us Allaah
being the unique, and the One who is intended
for completing the needs of everything and
everyone. As-Samad, who does not beget nor
was he begotten. It is not possible for anyone to
come with any other meaning.

As for the meaning of **Mutashabih** is every verse
in the Quran that carries numerous meanings
like Allaah's statement about Isa (ﷺ) –peace
be upon him,

﴿ وَكَلِمَتُهُۥٓ أَلْقَىٰهَآ إِلَىٰ مَرْيَمَ وَرُوحٌ مِّنْهُ ﴾

**"His word that he bestowed on Mary and a
spirit created by him"** [13]

---

[13] An-Nisaa [4: 171]

The word created in **"a spirit created by him"** is considered and ambiguous verse because the word by (*min*) in Arabic which is used by the Arab to mean three things:

1) Initiate form/ begin from

2) Part of

3) Clarification

Because these three meanings can be used in this verse it falls into **Mutashabih** "ambiguous verses". The Muslims found verses like this one to be ambiguous, so they applied this verse just as Allaah ordered in His statement,

﴿ مِنْهُ ءَايَتٌ مُّحْكَمَتٌ هُنَّ أُمُّ ٱلْكِتَبِ وَأُخَرُ مُتَشَبِهَتٌ ﴾

"From it are clear verses, they are the majority of the book and others are ambiguous" 14

So they returned the **Mutashabih** "ambiguous" back to the **Muh'kam** "clear verses" in his statement the Mighty and Sublime,

﴿ إِنَّ مَثَلَ عِيسَىٰ عِندَ ٱللَّهِ كَمَثَلِ ءَادَمَ خَلَقَهُۥ مِن تُرَابٍ ثُمَّ قَالَ لَهُۥ كُن فَيَكُونُ ﴿٥٩﴾ ﴾

---

14 Ali Imraan [3:7]

"Indeed the example of Isa with Allaah is like the example of Adam He created him from dirt then he said to him be, and it is" [15]

And the second verse,

﴿إِنْ هُوَ إِلَّا عَبْدٌ أَنْعَمْنَا عَلَيْهِ﴾

"He is nothing more than a slave that we have bestowed our grace upon" [16]

With these two clear verses it becomes clear "by" (*min*) in the verse *"created by him"* means initiated from and is not "part of" as the Christian Arabs claimed when they came to the Prophet ﷺ –forgiveness and safety be upon him- saying: *"We found in your book that was revealed to you, that which we claim about Isa (Jesus) to be true"*. He said to them:

"Where is this verse that you have?"

They said: Allaah says in your Book that He revealed to you,

"A spirit created by him," They said: " *by" (min) here is "part of" and we Arabs use" by" (min) to mean part of something. Therefore, Isa is a part of*

---

[15] Ali Imraan [3:59]
[16] Az-zukhruf [43:59].

Allaah and therefore, he (Jesus) is the son of Allaah.”

For this reason, Allaah says about the likes of them,

﴿ فَأَمَّا ٱلَّذِينَ فِى قُلُوبِهِمْ زَيْغٌ فَيَتَّبِعُونَ مَا تَشَٰبَهَ مِنْهُ ٱبْتِغَآءَ ٱلْفِتْنَةِ وَٱبْتِغَآءَ تَأْوِيلِهِۦ ۖ وَمَا يَعْلَمُ تَأْوِيلَهُۥٓ إِلَّا ٱللَّهُ وَٱلرَّٰسِخُونَ فِى ٱلْعِلْمِ ﴾

"And for those who has misguidance in their heart, they follow what is ambiguous from it (Quran). Desiring fitnah and to falsely interpret it (Quran) No one knows its interpretation but Allah and those who are firmly grounded in knowledge" [17]

Based on one of the two recitations for this verse:

The first of the two recitals: is linking without stopping in one verse **"wasl"** in His statement the Mighty and Sublime *"and no one knows its interpretation but Allaah and those firmly grounded in knowledge"* **"wasl"** which is linking the verse without stopping.

The second recital: *"And no one knows its interpretation but Allaah"* you pause here and then you recite *"and those firmly grounded in knowledge. They say we believe in it.*

---

[17] Ali Imraan [3:7]

Each one of these two types of recitals has
different meanings from one another. As far as
the:

1. **First Recital:** is "linking without stopping"
   here the word **"interpretation"** means
   explanation.

As for the:

2. **Second Recital:** is "stopping or pausing"
   and the meaning of **"interpretation"** here is
   how the true reality and essence of it is.

Second meaning, no one knows it except Allaah
and those firmly grounded in knowledge do not
know it at all. After the first meaning that
stemmed from **"wasl"** -linking without stopping-
were in interpretation means explanation, then
those firmly grounded in knowledge knows it, so
from this we realize that **Muh'kam** "clear" and
Mutashabih "ambiguous" verses fall into the
categories of "promises" and "threats".

The poet's statement: *"stories"* the stories of the
Quran are two categories:

1. Examples of the righteous: This enters
   into the "promise"

2. Examples of the non-righteous: This
   enters into "threats"

And the poet's statement *"admonition"* means reminders, and reminders are either "promises" or "threats", and his statement "examples" are examples in the Quran. The examples in the Quran are also two categories:

1. Examples for the righteous: This enters into the "promise"

2. Examples for the unrighteous: This enters into the "threats"

Therefore, those nine matters that are included in the poem enter under the three matters which are:

1. Tawheed
2. Tarheeb; wa'd
3. Targheeb: wa'eed

And all of them (the poet's statement and the author's statement) mean the same thing.

With this analogy, it becomes clear for us that the Quran is limited to these three matters that are included in Suratul-Fatihah in an eloquent manner that makes this chapter proceed forward like an obvious sign.

Here is a question that is necessary for one to ask: *'We heard you say in the beginning of your words: Al-fatihah includes Tawheed, Targheeb, and Tarheeb, where?"*

The answer by the success of Allaah -The Exalted- is His statement,

$$\text{﴿ ٱهْدِنَا ٱلصِّرَٰطَ ٱلْمُسْتَقِيمَ ۝ صِرَٰطَ ٱلَّذِينَ أَنْعَمْتَ عَلَيْهِمْ غَيْرِ ٱلْمَغْضُوبِ عَلَيْهِمْ وَلَا ٱلضَّآلِّينَ ۝ ﴾}$$

"Guide us to the straight path, the path of those whom you have bestowed your grace upon, not the path of those who have a wrath upon them, or those who are astray".

These words contain two matters:

The first matter: "Targheeb" is an encouragement to the straight path (The path of those whom Allaah has favored them of the prophets, extremely truthful, martyrs, and The Righteous). This is Targheeb.

The second matter: "Tarheeb" (frightening/causing fear) away from the path of those who have a wrath upon them and those who are astray. In addition to that this Surah contains the sciences of the Quran which breaks off into two other categories also:

1.praise and commandments to Allaah in the beginning.

2.The last part of the Surah teaches us to ask him, how do we supplicate based upon what the needs necessitate at different times just as Allaah says "With the name of Allaah the most merciful the most compassionate, All praise is due to Allaah lord of all that exists, Owner of the Day of Reckoning You alone we worship and seek aid.

All of this is praise and commandments to Allaah with His beautiful and lofty attributes that which no one has the right of worship but Him. What is the secret behind this chapter beginning with praise? The secret is that Allaah teaches us supplication and manners of asking as if He is saying to us: "When you supplicate and ask of me proceed in front of that -praise of Allaah- and the most excellent praise of Allaah is the praise that he praises himself within his Surah whereas he said:

"All praise is due to Allaah Lord of all that exists the most compassionate and merciful, Owner of the Day of Reckoning".

This is the most excellent praise, and Allaah loves being praised, so he glorifies himself and he did not leave charge of how to praise him to anyone else. Rather he glorified Himself first, and then He teaches us how to praise Him as comes in the narration,

مَا مِنْ أَحَدٍ أَحَبُّ إِلَيْهِ الْمَدْحُ مِنَ اللهِ

"There is no one being glorified is more beloved to him than Allah" [18]

Allaah –the glorified- loves to be praised and lauded by His servants. Therefore, He taught us how to glorify Him in the beginning of this chapter.

As far as it being inclusive to Tawheed; When you read this chapter, the first thing you encounter in it is Tawheed,

"All praise is due to Allah lord of all that exists".

This is Tawheed in lordship that the scholars of Tawheed named it: Unity (Tawheed) of sovereignty, unity in creation, unity of the dominion, and Tawheed of causing life (Ihyaa) and death (Imaatah) and other names.

This type of Tawheed is singling out Allaah alone in his actions. We isolate Him as being the sole creator or, master (of the universe and beyond). Owner (of it), causer of life and death, causer of

---

[18] agreed upon. Al-Bukhari collected it (hadeeth #4634), and Muslim collected it (hadeeth #2760).

harm and others from the names that we single Him out alone with. This appellate is called *"unity of Allaah in lordship"*, creating, provisions, and causing life or death so recognize.

This aspect of Tawheed no one rejects and when someone rejects it because he is deluded. When you debate him or contradict him scrutinizing his delusion, you will find that he certainly does not reject this aspect of Tawheed (lordship), but he is just a pompous, self-centered arrogant person rejecting the truth, like pharaoh who said,

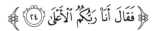

"I am your lord the most high" [19]

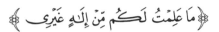

"I do not know for you a deity but me" [20]

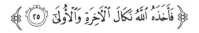

"So Allaah seized him with an exemplary punishment in the hereafter and this life"[21]

---

[19] An-Naazi'aat; [79:24]
[20] al-Qasas [28: 38]

This pompous said only two statements when Musa –on him and our prophet forgiveness and safety- talk back to him about it, and what did Allaah say about this in Surah-Nahl,

﴿لَقَدْ عَلِمْتَ مَاۤ أَنزَلَ هَـٰٓؤُلَاۤءِ إِلَّا رَبُّ ٱلسَّمَـٰوَٰتِ وَٱلْأَرْضِ﴾

"Truly, you know that no one prepared those things except the lord of the heavens and the earth" 22

Allaah has taken an oath by His might and Magnificence that the curse of Pharaoh and others who are pompous like him reject this aspect of Tawheed while he knows with certainty that Allaah is the lord of the heavens, earth, and that which is between them.

This statement in it the letter lam is prepared for an oath to be made that contains another hidden oath, implied oath as if Allaah is saying: *"By Allaah, truly you know O Pharaoh no one has prepared these things, but the lord of the heavens and the earth."* So for that reason the issue has become opposite of what Pharaoh said in his statement,

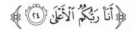

---

21 An-Naazi'aat [79:25]

22 Nahl [17:102]

"I am your lord the most high".[23]

Likewise, Allaah said about him in another verse in Surah Naml,

﴿وَجَحَدُوا۟ بِهَا وَٱسْتَيْقَنَتْهَآ أَنفُسُهُمْ ظُلْمًا وَعُلُوًّا فَٱنظُرْ كَيْفَ كَانَ عَـٰقِبَةُ ٱلْمُفْسِدِينَ ﴿١٤﴾﴾

"They (Pharaoh and his followers) rejected it (Tawheed in Lordship) out of oppression and arrogance, and they were certain of it within themselves so look at how the end was for the corruptors" [24]

Therefore, Tawheed Ar-Rububiyyah (unity in lordship) and sovereignty it is singling out Allah alone in his actions and there is no one who rejects this except an arrogant person. Everyone can be arrogant, but that arrogance disappears when argued and he becomes humiliated and becomes clear with debating him that he is nothing more than an arrogant pompous.

What is discovered about them sometimes is that they will call Allaah by other than His name. For example, sustenance, or Mother Nature, or essence and Allaah is totally free from what they say.

---

23 An-Naazi'aat [79:24]
24 An-Naml [27:14]

Or they may claim that what Pharaoh and Nimrod claimed or use whatever name they can find in the society they live in to reject this aspect of Tawheed.

As for a person living upon the realization that there is not a lord, creator, and provider, this does not exist at all. There only exists rejection of Allaah's names just as He says:

$$ \text{﴿ وَلِلَّهِ ٱلْأَسْمَآءُ ٱلْحُسْنَىٰ فَٱدْعُوهُ بِهَا ۖ وَذَرُوا ٱلَّذِينَ يُلْحِدُونَ فِىٓ أَسْمَٰٓئِهِۦ ﴾} $$

"And belongs to Allaah beautiful names so call on Him with them and leave those who reject His names" [25]

Meaning: they named him with other than His names and was pompous like Pharaoh -the cursed- was. This type of Tawheed (lordship) is also a means not a purpose, its natural disposition. Allaah says:

$$ \text{﴿ فِطْرَتَ ٱللَّهِ ٱلَّتِى فَطَرَ ٱلنَّاسَ عَلَيْهَا ﴾} $$

"This is the natural way of Allaah that He has originated mankind upon" [26]

---

[25] [Al-A'raaf [7:180]
[26] Ar-Room [30: 30]

If a child was born on the high part of a mountain and left there and Allaah decreed for him someone (without seeing him) to feed him and take care of his affairs only until he reached the age of discernment then you approach him while you are the first human being he encounters because he never went to a school before, just you ask him who is his lord, he will say to you **"Allaah is my lord"**.

This is the natural disposition Allaah has created that will never change or be altered just as the Prophet -forgiveness and peace of Allaah be upon him- said in the narration of Abu Hurairah,

كُلُّ مَوْلُودٍ عَلَى الْفِطْرَةِ ، أَبُوَاهُ يُهَدِّدَانِهِ أَوْ يُنَصِّرَانِهِ أَوْ يُمَدِّجِّسَانِهِ

"Every newborn is born on the Fitrah (natural belief of Allaah) then it is his parents that make him a Jew or a Christian or a Magician"
27

Meaning, a person does not turn away from Tawheed except with an evil education and upbringing. When a person is cultivated by someone who does not know Tawheed well, then every container exudes that which is in it. "If he

---

27 (agreed upon). Al-Bukhari collected it (hadeeth #1358), and Muslim collected (hadeeth 2658)

is a Jew, then exudes from him Judaism, if he is a Magician, then exudes from him is a Christian, if he is a Christian then exudes Christianity.

If Ashari Kilabi, then Kilabiyah, If Mu'tazilah, then I'tizaliyah, If Karami, then Karramiyah, if Hulooli, then Ghuloo and Ittihad, If fanatic upon a doctrine, then exude from him fanaticism blind following of doctrine. If a superstitious Sufi Philosopher who speak rhetoric, then exudes from him Sufism.

This type of Tawheed is not sufficient enough to enter Islam with at all, and every polytheist is aware of this category of Tawheed (lordship). This is the case with Abu Jahl, Abu Lahab, and others. What did Allaah say about these enemies? He said:

$$ \text{﴿ وَلَئِن سَأَلْتَهُم مَّنْ خَلَقَ ٱلسَّمَٰوَٰتِ وَٱلْأَرْضَ لَيَقُولُنَّ ٱللَّهُ ﴾} $$

"And if you were to ask them: Who created the heavens? They truly would say "Allaah" [28]

He also says:

$$ \text{﴿ قُلْ مَن رَّبُّ ٱلسَّمَٰوَٰتِ ٱلسَّبْعِ وَرَبُّ ٱلْعَرْشِ ٱلْعَظِيمِ ۝ سَيَقُولُونَ لِلَّهِ ﴾} $$

---

28 Luqman [31:25]

"Say who is the lord of the seven heavens, and the lord of the magnificent throne? They shall say " Allaah" [29]

Tawheed of lordship directs towards Unity in Allaah's worship out of necessity. **Meaning:** You acknowledging that Allaah is your lord, owner, creator, and provider, then this acknowledgement requires and necessitates that you worship the lord and single him out alone for worship just as the unity in the worship of Allaah (Tawheed Al Uloohiyyah) directs towards unity in Allaah's lordship inclusively. All that means is that you are worshipping this magnificent lord is with what He legislated and refraining from what He has prohibited. That is inclusive to His lordship because if you do not know His lordship, you would not worship him by complying with His commands and avoiding His prohibitions.

In regards to the following categories of Tawheed that He mentions in the Quran, the disbelievers rejects it saying about Tawheed Al-Uloohiyyah (singling out Allaah alone for worship) just as Allaah has informed about them,

﴿إِذَا قِيلَ لَهُمْ لَآ إِلَٰهَ إِلَّا ٱللَّهُ يَسْتَكْبِرُونَ ﴿٣٥﴾﴾

"When it is told to them there is no deity in truth but Allaah, they reject arrogantly" [30]

---

[29] al-Mu'minun [23:86-87].

And in another verse He says:

﴿ أَجَعَلَ ٱلْآلِهَةَ إِلَٰهًا وَٰحِدًا ﴾

"Is he making the deities, one deity" 31

Tawheed in Worship, they do not acknowledge it, and the proof is their talbiyyah (supplication made on the hajj) on (Hajj) Pilgrimage:

لَبَيْكَ، لَبَيْكَ لَا شَرِيكَ لَكَ إِلَّا شَرِيكًا هُوَ لَكَ، تَمْلِكُهُ وَ مَا مَلَكَ.

"Responding to you O Allaah responding to you, no partners for You but the partner that is for You, You own him and that which he possess" 32

They acknowledge lordship, dominion, creating, and providing is for Allaah. However they reject Allaah being the only deity worthy of worship and glorification. When it is said to them: "You acknowledge Allaah's lordship, then that should require you to acknowledge His right of being worshipped alone." They said:

---

30 As-Saafat [37: 3]
31 [Saad [38:5].
32 Look in: Saheeh Muslim (#1185)

$$\text{﴿ مَا نَعْبُدُهُمْ إِلَّا لِيُقَرِّبُونَا إِلَى اللَّهِ زُلْفَىٰ ﴾}$$

"We worship them only that they may bring us closer to Allaah in nearness"[33]

This is their corrupted call that Allaah has revoked.

From here it becomes very clear to us that Tawheed is the worship of Allah and Tawheed in His lordship do not have the same meaning like the Al-Ash'ariyyah Al-Kilabiyyah, Al-Hanifiyyah Al-Matrudiyyah, Al-karaamiyyah As-Sajastaaniyyah, and Al-Jahmiyyah Al-Ja'diyyah claims. Thus, you find all these groups from the people of Rhetoric and philosophy, those who have turned away from the Quran and the prophetic traditions and have occupied themselves with rhetoric and philosophy. Opinions solely based upon what appears to them around empty issues that have no correct results.

SECOND ASPECT OF TAWHEED: TAWHEED ASMAA WA SIFAAAT (UNITY IN NAMES AND ATTRIBUTES OF ALLAAH

Tawheed of Allaah's names and attributes is that which Allaah repeats in this Surah often in his statement:

"The Most Merciful and Compassionate • Owner of the Day of Reckoning."

Ar-Rahmaan (Merciful) and Ar-Raheem (Compassionate) are two names abstracted from the word Ar-Rahmān, (mercy) and Ar-Rahman is more intense of a meaning than Ar-Raheem. Ar-Rahmaan is for all of the creation, and Ar-Raheem is for the true believer just as He the Exalted said:

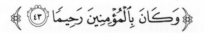

"And He (the messenger) was compassionate (Raheem) to the believers." 34

And his statement:

﴿ مَـٰلِكِ يَوْمِ ٱلدِّينِ ۝ ﴾

---

34 Al-Ahzaab [33:43]

"The Owner (Maalik) of The Day of Reckoning.

In it is, two types of the seven modes of recitations, any of them you recite are correct. It is correct to say: **"Owner of the day of reckoning."** Or **"King of the day of reckoning."** Just by dropping a letter 'a' in (Maalik) making it (Malik). The day of reckoning is: the day of recompense (Deen), which means:

"As you treat others you will be treated."

Meaning: as you do unto others will be done to you. For this reason, Islaam has been called the religion of Recompense (Deen) because whoever practices and implements it will obtain a good reward. Here, Allaah mentions three names from his 99 names that...

مَنْ أَحْصَاهَا دَخَلَ الْجَنَّةَ

"Whoever enumerates them enters Paradise"
35

Which Imam At-Tirmidhi brings in his Jami'.[36]

Ar-Rahman, Ar-Raheem, and Malik(King) of the Deen (Day of Recompense) he mentioned them

---

[35] Agreed upon. Al-Bukhari collects it (hadeeth 6410) and Muslim collects it (hadeeth 2677).
[36] At-tirmidhi collected it (hadeeth 3507).

as an example for Tawheed in Allaah's names and attributes. It is obligatory upon every person to believe in all of Allaah's beautiful names and attributes based on the three foundations Allaah mentions in his Wise Book.

Firstly: Affirming them

Secondly: Freeing them of any resemblance to his creation

Thirdly: Losing hope in comprehending how they truly are and the essence of them.

Allaah mentions all three foundations in his Wise Book. He mentions two foundations in Surah Ashura in his statement:

﴿لَيْسَ كَمِثْلِهِۦ شَيْءٌ وَهُوَ ٱلسَّمِيعُ ٱلْبَصِيرُ ۞﴾

"There is nothing liking unto Him and He is The All Hearing and Seeing." [37]

These two foundations rest upon Tawheed of Allaah's names and attributes.

Firstly: Freeing Allaah from resemblance to the creation in His self, Names, and Attributes based from the example in His statement:

---

[37] Ash-Ashura [42:11]

﴾ لَيْسَ كَمِثْلِهِ شَيْءٌ ﴿

"There is nothing liking unto Him."

Secondly: Affirming everything Allaah describes Himself with or named Himself with or what His Messenger (Forgiveness and Peace be upon Him) described Him or named Him with, just as it comes in His statement The Exalted:

﴾ وَهُوَ ٱلسَّمِيعُ ٱلْبَصِيرُ ۝ ﴿

"And He is the All Hearing and Seeing."

The third foundation is in Suratul Baqarah and Taha. As for Baqarah in Ayatul Kursi:

﴾ وَلَا يُحِيطُونَ بِشَيْءٍ مِّنْ عِلْمِهِ إِلَّا بِمَا شَآءَ ﴿

"They encompass nothing of his knowledge except what he wills" [38]

And in Surah Taha:

﴾ وَلَا يُحِيطُونَ بِهِ عِلْمًا ۝ ﴿

"They encompass nothing of knowledge." [39]

---

[38] Baqarah [2:255]
[39] Taha [20:11]

In these two verses are clear texts that it is not possible for the creation to encompass the knowledge of Allaah, and whoever tries to look into knowing how the self of Allaah is His attributes, and names truly he is looking into that which he has no capability at all to gain knowledge like that. So it is obligatory upon every human being to believe in these beautiful and Lofty attributes based on these three foundations even if he cannot know their true essence of them and how they truly are.

This is the case because the person who finds it strange to believe in the names and attributes without comprehending the true essence of them, then let him realize that there is something right in his own creation that he cannot truly get to the true essence of it but yet, he still believes in it, and that is the spirit that is within him. If you were asked about the true essence of it and how it is, you would be incapable of knowing its true reality. Therefore if you are unable to know the true essence of the human creation such as yourself then first and foremost you are incapable of knowing the true essence of the Names and Attributes and the Self of The Creator Allaah.

Do not be in regards to this aspect of Tawheed like the Mu'atilah (Those who negate the names and attributes of Allaah) nor the Mumathilah (Those who make the resemblance between the attributes of Allaah and His creations), rather be upon the balance between these two evil groups.

In addition to what proceeded, it is obligatory on every Muslim to avoid the three evils upon Tawheed in Allaah's Names and Attributes:

1).**Ta'teel** (rejection of the names and attributes)
2). **Ta'weel** (Falsely interpreting them)
3).**Tamtheel** (Resembling them to his creation)

These three لام **"Laams"**⁴⁰ (The three categories) are from the rejections of these categories of Tawheed. Every Muslim must avoid these things in relation to Tawheed and must avoid everyone who has strayed in this subject; the reason is because of him being attached to one of these rejecters.

Likewise, it is obligatory upon every Muslim and human being who believes in Allaah to avoid the three evil جيم **"Jeems"**, and they are:

1). The **Jeem** in Jahm in the attributes of Allaah
2). The **Jeem** in Jabr in the actions of Allaah
3). The **Jeem** in Irjaa in Belief

So every Muslim must avoid the three **"Laams"** and the three **"Jeems"**.

---

⁴⁰ **Meaning;** from disbelief regarding Allaah's names and attributes.

We will stop here to take a moment to explain what Ta'weel is since there is a need for that to be mentioned here and clarify this evil understanding that the people of rhetoric and philosophy have made terminologies based from this Ta'weel. We say Ta'weel has three meanings:

First meaning: is Tafseer (explanation) just as Allaah says:

$$﴿ هَٰذَا تَأْوِيلُ رُءْيَٰىَ مِن قَبْلُ ﴾$$

"This is the Ta'weel (explanation) of my dream before" [41]

Meaning: (this is) the Tafseer of my dream before.

Also, among it (i.e., Its proofs) is the narration of Aishah –May Allaah Be Pleased with Her- That the Prophet ﷺ –Forgiveness and Blessings be upon Him- used to say in his prostration:

$$سُبْحَانَكَ اللَّهُمَّ وَ بِحَمْدِكَ، اللَّهُمَّ اغْفِرْ لِي$$

"O Allaah glory to you by your praise, O Allaah I beg you to forgive me,"

He made Ta'weel (explanation) of the Quran." [42]

---

[41] Yusuf [12:100]

Aisha meant by her statement: *"He made interpretation of the Quran,"* **meaning:** He explained to us the words in Surah An-Nasr,

"So with the praises of your Lord and seek His forgiveness." [43]

Also, among it (i.e., Its proofs) is the statement of Ibn Jareer in his noble explanation of the Quran, which there is nothing like it in explanation to the Quran. He said many times:

"The statement in regards to the Ta'weel (explanation) of this verse."

Meaning: Tafseer of this verse, so this is the first meaning for Ta'weel.

Second meaning: Ta'weel **means** the reality of something and this type of meaning only Allaah knows. This is what is intended in His statement based upon one of the two recitations in the previous verse we recited,

﴿ وَمَا يَعْلَمُ تَأْوِيلَهُ إِلَّا اللَّهُ ﴾

---

[42] Agreed upon. Al-Bukhari collected it (hadeeth 817) and Muslim collected it (hadeeth 484).
[43] An-Nasir [110:3]

"And No One knows the interpretation of it except Allaah." [44]

Here is a place of pausing and stopping. So Ta'weel based on this recitation means the reality of a thing.

(Next Proof) is from His (i.e., Allaah) statement:

$$ هَلْ يَنظُرُونَ إِلَّا تَأْوِيلَهُ ۚ $$

"They do not wait for anything but its reality (ta'weel) to unfold." [45]

No one knows the reality of what will happen on the Day of Judgment, Paradise, Hell, The Bridge, The Fountain, and other things from what Allaah has mentioned in His Wise Book, no one knows the reality of them save Allaah.

As for the meanings and explanations of the Quran it is well known to the Arabs because it is their language, likewise the scholars who study this clear book know the explanation.

From here we understand that which our brother from the Ash-Ariyah Al-Kilabiyah and the Al-Hanifiyyah Al-Matrudiyyah say: *"There is something called ambiguous verses (Mutashabih) that no one knows from mankind their meanings*

---

[44] Ali Imraan [3:7]
[45] A'raaf [7:53]

that are in the Quran or Sunnah." This
statement is the highest level of corruption.

It is not possible for it to exist, neither in the
Book (Quran) nor the Sunnah a word that the
Arabs and scholars of Islam do not know the
meaning of.

Truly that which exist in the Quran and the
Sunnah that is ambiguous are relatively
ambiguous, meaning that there are verses or
words in the Quran that some scholars know
their meanings and others do not. So this is
what we call **"relatively ambiguous"**.

Some can relate to its meanings and others
cannot because Allaah's tradition with regard to
His creation is that he made them vary in virtue,

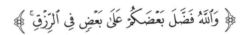

**"And Allaah has made some of you more
virtuous than other in provisions." 46**

So this scholar may know the meaning of a verse
and another scholar does not. This is something
that everyone confirms and agrees on.

As far as the scholars all agree on is that they all
do not know the meaning of a particular verse or
word, then this is impossible to exist.

---

46 Nahl [16:71]

Perhaps this person gauges others based on his self and this type of measuring is corrupted because he has made two doors into one door and it is not permissible for you to judge with what you judge yourself with.

If you are ignorant to this matter, does that necessitate me to be ignorant of that?! No, it is not necessary.

As for the **Third meaning** then it is innovative interpretation, false interpretation, which causes a serious setback in the creed of philosophers and the people of rhetoric which is altering from their obvious meanings to another definition by using a claimed proof that prevent usage of the intended first meaning.

This Ta'weel with this consideration could be correct or wrong; however, the majority of the time it is wrong or falsehood. This is because it is the way the Jews, disbelievers, Mulhidoon (those who reject the names and attributes of Allaah), and the mutazandiqoon (those who intentionally accept Islam for the purpose of destroying it from within). So It is not permissible for any Muslim to argue with the likes of this category (of ta'weel).

It is the second Taaghoot (false deity) that Ibn Qayyim ﷻ concluded with in his book *"As Sawaai'q"* into two categories:

1. **First Taaghoot:** Implied meaning

2. **Second Taaghoot:** It is a false interpretation with the meaning I mentioned.

Statement of Allaah the Exalted:

$$﴿ إِيَّاكَ نَعْبُدُ وَإِيَّاكَ نَسْتَعِينُ ۝ ﴾$$

"You alone we worship and you alone we seek help."

Meaning: we do not worship anyone, but you. This is called in Arabic language **"Hasr"** (i.e., Enclosure) which is well known in the language, and it has four tools (words to do that enclosure)

1. Give precedence to the thing the action will be applied to like here.

2. Enclosure with using إلّا **"Illa"** (i.e., Except).

3. Enclosure with using the word إنَّمَا **"Innama"** (i.e., Truly).

4. Enclosure with using a conjunction like:

$$جَاءَ زَيْدٌ لَا عَمْرُو$$

"Zaid came, <u>not</u> Amr."

The **"Balaaghiyyun"** (i.e., Scholars of eloquence) have written a text even though their eloquence can be criticized it still have with it beneficial affairs that are necessary for the student of knowledge to be familiar with.

They say: *"And the tools of enclosure are "illa" and "innama" and giving precedence to the thing the action is applied to."*

The point is that when the **Ma'mool**[47] is mentioned before its **'Aamil**[48] then the **"Hasr"** (i.e., Enclosure) is implied. Example:

$$ ﴿ إِيَّاكَ نَعْبُدُ ﴾ $$

"You alone we worship." [49]

Many verses are mentioned like this in the Quran. Like his statement:

$$ ﴿ ۞ وَقَضَىٰ رَبُّكَ أَلَّا تَعْبُدُوٓا۟ إِلَّآ إِيَّاهُ ﴾ $$

---

[47] **PN**: This term in Arabic is referring to who or what an action is occurred to it, whether it occurs through a verb and its object or what occurs between a subject and its predicate.

[48] **PN:** This term in Arabic refers to a noun or verb that causes object change its vowel ending.

[49] **TN**: meaning the words *"you alone"* comes before the action verb *"we worship"* indicate enclosure since the name of Allaah is mentioned first before the action which is Him showing us how to single Him out alone for worship in our statements).

"And your lord has decreed that you do not worship anyone save Him alone" [50]

Meaning: *laa ilaha illa Allaah*. No deity deserves to be worshipped from all aspects of worship except Allaah because He is the lord, Master, King, Creator, Provider, Benefactor, Causer of harm, and other than that from His 99 names and attributes that whoever enumerate them he enters paradise.

If you were to follow all the verses that mention this meaning, you would write a medium size volume. No speech or words get this type of concern except the speech of Allaah in His Wise Book,

$$ ﴿ وَمَا خَلَقْتُ ٱلْجِنَّ وَٱلْإِنسَ إِلَّا لِيَعْبُدُونِ ۝ ﴾ $$

"I did not create mankind and jinkind save to worship me (alone)" [51]

Since this continues to remain the purpose (of creation) then these verses and words deserve this type of concern over anything else.

The meaning of Uloohiyah: is 'Ibaadah (i.e., Worship). This is the meaning that the Arabs know from their speech; if you do not know the speech of the Arabs then surely you are far away

---

[50] al-Israa [17:23]
[51] Adh-Dhariyaat [51:56]

from knowing the explanation of the Quran. That is why Ibn Abbaas said – Allaah be pleased with him- from that which Al-Bayhaqi narrates in his (book) **"Shu'ba"**, He said,

"Upon you are collections of the Arabs because in them are the meanings your book (Quran)." [52]

Al-Arabi said in regards to the meaning of Uloohiyyah (worship):

لله دَرُّ الْغَانِيَاتِ الْمُدَّهِ

سَبَّحْنَ وَاسْتَرْجَعْنَ مِنْ تَأَلُّهِي

"Amazing is how beautifully women singing are so astonished how my worship comes between me inclining toward their beauty." [53]

Tawheed Uloohiyah (unity of the worship of Allaah) is the third of the categories of Tawheed that Allaah has made a text for it in His statement:

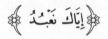

﴿ إِيَّاكَ نَعْبُدُ ﴾

"You alone we worship"

---

[52] Look in the book: *"Al- Jami' li shu'abu Eemaan"* (vol. 4/ page 316, #1560).

[53] The line of poetry is by Ru'bah bin Al-'Ujaaj in his collection of poetry: *"Majmoo Ashar Al-'Arab"* page 165.

Which is the goal and greatest purpose illustrated in this verse, and it means **La ilaha illa Allaah meaning:** No deity in truth but Allaah. Everyone that you worship other than Him the glorified, then that worship is invalid and thrown back in your face because it has occurred in the wrong place.

For that reason Allaah has called this form of worship oppression in His statement in Surah An'am,

$$\text{﴿ ٱلَّذِينَ ءَامَنُوا۟ وَلَمْ يَلْبِسُوٓا۟ إِيمَٰنَهُم بِظُلْمٍ ﴾}$$

"Those who believe and do not cover their belief with oppression (shirk)." [54]

Why is shirk (polytheism) called oppression?

That is because polytheism is placing worship in the wrong place. Whoever worships other than Allaah, an angel, prophet, tree, rock, mud, substance, or nature truly this person has placed worship in its wrong place and that is why Allaah called it oppression.

Oppression: Is placing something in the wrong place.

It is well-known that whoever commits this act of worship for other than Allaah has initiated an

---

[54] Al-'An'am [6:82.]

act of oppression. This reason Allaah, the mighty and sublime, said in another verse in Baqarah:

﴿وَٱلْكَٰفِرُونَ هُمُ ٱلظَّٰلِمُونَ ۝٢٥٤﴾

"The Disbelievers are oppressors." 55

When one of the Tabi'een (followers of the companions of the Prophet) heard this noble verse he said:

لَكَ الْـحَـمْـدُ يَا رَبِّ ، حَيْثُ قُلْتَ : ﴿وَٱلْكَٰفِرُونَ هُمُ ٱلظَّٰلِمُونَ

۝٢٥٤﴾ ،وَ لَـمْ تَـقُـلْ : وَ الـظَّـالِـمِـيـنَ هُـمُ الْـكَـافِـرِيـنَ .

"Belongs to you all the praise O my lord. Were as you "The disbelievers are oppressors." And you did not say: And the oppressors are the disbelievers. 56

If He (Allaah) said: **"And the oppressors are the disbelievers"** then who is safe from his disbelief?!

Look at this tremendous understanding. The understanding is not something in the hands of

---

55 Baqarah [2:253]
56 Ibn Jareer collected similar to it in his tafseer (3/4), and ibn Abi Hatim in his tafseer (2/485) both of its chain of narration is attributed to the statement of Atah Ibn Dinnar in the tafseer Of Ibn Jareer.

a person that he can place it in the heart of another person, rather it is something that Allaah prefers to give to whom He pleases among His servants for reasons he has made clear in His Book and in the authentic narration that is narrated by Mu'aawiyah - may Allaah be pleased with him,

مَنْ يُرِدِ اللهُ بِهِ خَيْرًا يُفَقِّهْهُ فِي الـدِّينِ

"Whoever Allaah intends good for, He gives him understanding of the religion." [57]

Let's stop here briefly with this verse because some people present an issue with this verse.

Some people say, *"It is customarily well known that means (that which is used to arrive at a purpose) always come before purposes, and in this noble verse:*

﴿ إِيَّاكَ نَعْبُدُ وَإِيَّاكَ نَسْتَعِينُ ٥ ﴾

"You alone we worship and seek assistance."

Comes the opposite with the purpose being mentioned before the means so what is the secret behind that and the destroying of this principle along with knowing that if we were to investigate the Noble Quran we would find this principle all

---

[57] Agreed upon; Al-Bukhari collected it (hadeeth 17) and Muslim (hadeeth 1037).

*through it so again what is the secret behind
that?"*

Answer: The secret behind it are two affairs:

The first matter: is proceeding the right of
Allaah over human rights

The second matter: is indicating the
significance of the main purpose (Allaah) which
is greatest purpose and goal just as it comes in
the verse of Surah Adh-Dhariyat:

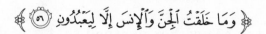

" I have not created jinkind and mankind
save to worship me" [58]

What is meant by preceding Allaah's rights over
human rights is that worship is the right of
Allaah and seeking aid is the right of mankind
Along with the fact seeking assistance is a
means to worship.

Except here, worship has a preference over
seeking help and assistance to indicate the
importance of the goal (Allaah) and that it is the
greatest purpose and purest right of Allaah. This
is what the scholars of research and
investigation comprehend about this subject
which comes from striving hard to understand

---

[58] Adh-Dhariyaat [51:56]

the Book of Allaah. We previously mentioned the statement of Allaah:

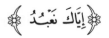

"You alone we worship."

Is an expression about the **Word of Sincerity** (La Ilaha Illa Allaah), like in Allaah's statement, The Mighty and Sublime, in the verse:

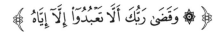

"And your Lord has decreed that you do not worship anyone save him alone." [59]

Until the end of it is an explanation and clarification for the meaning of **"La Ilaha Illa Allaah Muhammad Rasoolullah"** (There is a deity in truth except Allaah; Muhammad is the Messenger of Allaah)".

These words have weight and value that no other value equal to it because none can, as you know, enter the folds of Islam except with these words that contain two parts:

Part One: There is no God in truth but Allaah. **Meaning:** singling out Allaah alone for all forms of worship and no one else.

---

[59] Al-Isra [17:23]

Part Two: Muhammad is the Messenger of Allaah. **Meaning**: singling out this Noble Prophet (ﷺ) with following him and no one else from the creation.

This is the Tawheed that the messengers all were sent with:

﴿ وَمَا خَلَقْتُ ٱلْجِنَّ وَٱلْإِنسَ إِلَّا لِيَعْبُدُونِ ٥٦ ﴾

"I have not created jinkind nor mankind except to worship me." [60]

Meaning: single Him out alone with worship, and to single out alone His Messenger for following, Allaah says:

﴿ مَّن يُطِعِ ٱلرَّسُولَ فَقَدْ أَطَاعَ ٱللَّهَ ﴾

"Whoever obeys the messenger has truly obeyed Allaah." [61]

And He said:

﴿ وَإِن تُطِيعُوهُ تَهْتَدُواْ ﴾

"If you obey him you will be guided." [62]

---

[60] Adh-Dhariyat [51:56]
[61] An-Nisaa [4:80]

He also said:

﴿ وَمَآ ءَاتَىٰكُمُ ٱلرَّسُولُ فَخُذُوهُ وَمَا نَهَىٰكُمْ عَنْهُ فَٱنتَهُواْ ﴾

"What the Messenger give you take it! And what He prohibits leave it." [63]

In an authentic narration from the narration of Anas- may Allaah be pleased with him.

لَا يُؤْمِنُ أَحَدُكُمْ حَتَّى أَكُونَ أَحَبَّ إِلَيْهِ مِنْ وَالِدِهِ وَ
وَلَدِهِ وَ النَّاسِ أَجْمَعِينَ .

"None of you truly believes until I am more be love to him than his parents, children and all of mankind." [64]

At any rate, following the Prophet ﷺ is obligatory like the obligation of worshiping Allaah alone because following The Messenger ﷺ is obedience and worship to Allaah. Just like what Allaah, the mighty and sublime, stipulated in many verses. Among them is His statement:

---

[62] An-Nur [24:54]
[63] Al-Hashr [59:7]
[64] Agreed upon, Al-Bukhari collected it (hadeeth 15) and Muslim collected it (hadeeth 44).

﴿ فَلْيَحْذَرِ ٱلَّذِينَ يُخَالِفُونَ عَنْ أَمْرِهِۦٓ أَن تُصِيبَهُمْ فِتْنَةٌ أَوْ يُصِيبَهُمْ عَذَابٌ
أَلِيمٌ ۝ ﴾

"Let beware those who opposes his commandment that will befall them a trial or befall them a painful chastisement." [65]

What is the trial that is feared upon whoever opposes a statement, action, and confirmation of the Prophet ﷺ for the sake of blind following someone's opinion or the culture of his society, environment, father, or his sheikh. What is this trial that is feared upon this individual?

Truly Imam Ahmad Ibn Hanbal, clarified it when he was asked, *"what is fitnah (trials)? He said: Shirk (polytheism).* [66]

Meaning: that the person, who gives precedence to someone's opinion, whoever that may be, over the Prophets statement, actions, and his conformation this means that he doubts in the message of The Prophet ﷺ, and if he was certain and unwavering about his Message ﷺ truly would not have preceded the options of anyone over his statements, action, and confirmation no matter whom it is whether it be his father, ruler, society, or his

---

[65] An-Nur [24:63]
[66] Ibn Batta collected it in his book *"al-Ibaanah Kubraa"* (1/260) with its chain of narrators to Al-Fadil bin Ziyaad from Imam Ahmad.

environment. The statement of Allaah, the Exalted:

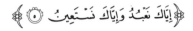

"You alone we worship and seek aid."

Indicates two types of Tawheed:

First Tawheed: Tawheed Uloohiyah (unity in the worship of Allah alone.)

Second Tawheed: Tawheed Mutaba'ah (unity in following the Prophet).[67]

The meaning of Tawheed Uloohiyyah: is Unity of Allaah in His worship in all of its aspects whereas none of it is disposed for other than Allaah: like prayer, alms-giving, fasting, pilgrimage, vows, slaughtering, seeking aid, seeking rescue, fear, trust, and other than that from the numerous aspects of worship.

Rather, you dispose all of it for Allaah, the mighty and sublime; and with that you remove yourself from Polytheism on all levels.

The meaning of Tawheed Mutaba'ah: Singling out the noble Prophet ﷺ alone for following him and no one else from the creation,

---

[67] Among those who stipulates this is Al-'Allamah Ibn Qayyim in his book: "Madarij As-Salikeen" (2/387).

and mentioning the proof for it come later. Many authors and students of knowledge shorten Tawheed to just three categories (Tawheed Ruboobiyah, Uloohiyah, and Asmaa wa Sifaat), and it does not mean there is not a fourth category as some would think. Rather the fourth category of Tawheed whether we mention it or not it already exists within the three.

The fourth category: Tawheed Mutaba'ah.

Meaning: singling out the Prophet ﷺ for following him and no one else from the creation. This is because no other prophet was sent to us other than him.

The proofs for this aspect of Tawheed are many verses some have preceded the mentioning of them and sufficient enough as proof for it is the **Testimony of Sincerity,** and it has two parts:

First Part: There is no God in Truth save Allaah.

Second Part: Muhammad is the Messenger of Allaah.

The first part: is Tawheed of worship **meaning:** 'Ibaadah. **The second part:** is Tawheed of following by singling out the Prophet ﷺ for following him and no one else from the creation, like Allaah said:

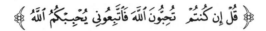

"Say: If you love Allaah then follow me. Allaah will love you." [68]

Likewise, the first part is also "the word of Sincerity, *"which is unity of Allaah in his worship,"* **meaning:** singling out Allaah alone for worship less than anyone or thing from the creation whether that be a Prophet, Angel, or messenger of any type. Worship is for Allaah alone with all its many categories that are clarified in the book of Allaah and the traditions of His Messenger ﷺ .

The reason that these two forms of Tawheed are inclusive to the "word of Sincerity". Which is "There is no God in Truth, but Allaah and that Muhammad is the Messenger of Allaah, is that they are necessarily tied together forever, never to be separated, and one cannot be independent of the other.

Whoever says, **La Ilaha illa Allaah** without saying **Muhammadur Rasoolullah** would not have entered into Islam at all. Likewise, the one who says **Muhammad Rasoolullah** without saying, **Laa Ilaha Illa Allaah** did not enter Islam either. Therefore from here the scholars comprehend that these two words that when one of them is individualized in the Quran or the

---

68 Ali Imraan [3:31]

Sunnah it enters automatically into the other. So Allaah's statement...

$$﴿ فَاعْلَمْ أَنَّهُ لَا إِلَهَ إِلَّا اللَّهُ ﴾$$

"Know! That there is no God in truth save Allaah." [69]

...doesn't mean that you say that only and that is sufficient, no! Rather it means just as our Prophet ﷺ explained in the authentic narration:

$$أُمِرْتُ أَنْ أُقَاتِلَ النَّاسَ حَتَّى يَشْهَدُوا: أَنْ لَا إِلَهَ إِلَّا اللهُ، وَ أَنِّي رَسُولُ اللهِ.$$

"I have been commanded to fight the people until they testify There is no God in truth save Allaah and that I am the messenger of Allaah." [70]

So when one of these two words are mentioned in the Quran by itself it automatically enters into the other even if it is not mentioned. Likewise, that, which is like, it in the Quran the words:

✓ **Miskeen**(very poor) and **Faqeer** (poor)

---

[69] Muhammad [47:19]
[70] Agreed upon from the hadeeth ibn 'Umar, may Allaah be pleased with them both. Al-Bukhari collected it (hadeeth 25) and Muslim collected it (hadeeth 22).

- ✓ **Birr** (righteousness) and **Taqwa** (piety)
- ✓ **Ithm** (sin) and **Udwan**(transgression)
- ✓ **Istighfaar** (seeking forgiveness) and **Tawba** (repentance)
- ✓ **Kufr** (disbelief) and **Nifaq** (hypocrisy).

When these words and their likes are isolated without the other, enters into it the other, and when they are mentioned together their meanings differ in meaning, and when they are individualized they mean the same as the other.

The proof is the narration of Jabreel [71] عَلَيْهِ السَّلَامُ. Within it is mentioned Islam and Eemaan, and each one have a meaning different from the other. Islam means when gathered with Eemaan: obvious actions and Eemaan means hidden actions and Ihsaan (excellence) has two positions or standards.

When Eemaan is, mentioned by itself in the narration of the party of Abdul Qais who, within the it (i.e., Hadeeth) accepted Islam when the Prophet صَلَّى اللهُ عَلَيْهِ وَسَلَّمَ said to them:

أَ تَدْرُونَ مَا الْإِيمَانُ؟ قَالُوا لَهُ: اللهُ وَ رَسُولُهُ أَعْلَمُ،

قَالَ: الْإِيمَانُ أَنْ تَشْهَدُوا أَنْ لَا إِلَهَ إِلَّا اللهُ، وَ أَنَّ مُحَمَّدًا

---

[71] Al-Bukhari collected it (#50) and Muslim collected it (#9) from the hadeeth Abi Hurairah, may Allaah be pleased with him.

رَسُولُ اللهِ ، وَ تُقِيمُوا الصَّلَاةَ ، وَ تُؤْتُوا الزَّكَاةَ ، وَ

تُؤَدُّوا الْخُمُسَ مِنَ الْمَغْنَمِ .

"Do you know what Eemaan is?" They said:
"Allaah and His Messenger know best." He said:
**"Eemaan is to testify that there is no God in
truth but Allaah and that Muhammad
Messenger of Allaah, That charity, and you
give a fifth of the war booty."** [72]

This narration includes in it Islam and Eemaan
together. This is the case because establishing
the prayer and giving charity is from Islam,
likewise performing a fifth (i.e., Of the war booty)
is from Islam like what we presented in the
narration of Jabreel ﷺ **Islam** is outwardly
actions and **Eemaan** is hidden actions.

With this, it is understood that Islam and
Eemaan when they are mentioned gather their
meanings then differ and when they come
individually it takes the meaning of the other.

That is also the same with the *"word of sincerity"*
when its first half is mentioned (La Ilaaha
IllaAllaah) which is Tawheed of worship enters in
it Tawheed Mutaba'ah, likewise, if Tawheed-ul-
Mutaba'ah (Muhammad is the Messenger of

---

[72] Agreed upon from the narrations of Ibn Abbas. Al-Bukhari
collected it (hadeeth 53) and Muslim collected it (hadeeth 17).

Allaah) is mentioned alone enters into it Tawheed of worship.

Categorizing Tawheed with another consideration Tawheed is categorized into two other considered categories:

1. General Tawheed
2. Specific Tawheed

General Tawheed: that which is comprehended by verses related to actions (i.e., Allaah's actions).

Specific Tawheed: That which is comprehended by verses related to statements.

General Tawheed: is comprehended, by verses related to actions is Tawheed of Lordship (Ruboobiyah).

Verses related to actions: are the heavens and earth and what is between them, and by looking at the creation, you can deduct from that there is for this creation a magnificent Lord described with beautiful complete attributes; and this is possible for everyone to understand because it is a natural disposition.

Specific Tawheed that Allaah, the mighty and sublime, clarified in this Surah (Fatihah), then it is not possible to understand it by any means except by verses related to statements, which are the Quran and Sunnah.

As for philosophy and the science of Rhetoric, then they have no share what so ever in the science of Tawheed at all.

Why, because no one can teach the attributes of Allaah, but Allaah and the Messenger of Allaah  whom Allaah taught, and Allaah knows best about himself than anyone from the creation.

Therefore, philosophic and rhetoric are newly introduced affairs into Islam. It (i.e., Islam) does not know of it; rather Islam rejects and invalidate Philosophic and rhetoric.

ᏕᎧ ✹ ✹ ✹ ᏩᎡ

STATEMENT OF ALLAAH- THE EXALTED: "GUIDE US TO THE STRAIGHT PATH"

Statement of Allaah, the exalted,

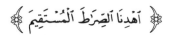

"Guide us to the straight path."

This is a supplication; that is the most inclusive and beneficial supplication. There does not exist in the Quran nor the Sunnah a single supplication more inclusive and beneficial than this supplication. So for that reason Allaah, the mighty and sublime, taught us it.

And the meaning of...

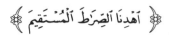

"Guide us to the straight path."

Means: *"O' Our Lord, whom we praise with that which He has taught us, we ask and call upon You with this supplication that You have taught us that You guide us to the straight path."*

Guidance to the straight path **means:** That You teach us what benefits us and You (i.e., Allaah) grant us success to implement what will benefit us. The word *"Guide us."* Includes two matters:

First Matter: Guidance means being directed to beneficial knowledge.

Second Matter: Guidance towards acting according to the beneficial knowledge. So *"Guide us"* **means** Grant us success towards beneficial knowledge, which is the Quran and Sunnah, righteous deeds, which is implementing the Quran and Sunnah.

As for practicing innovation, superstitious beliefs, and purely unfounded opinions of men then this is not from righteous acts; rather, it is from unrighteous deeds.

Righteous deeds are those deeds that apply to three verses from the Book of Allaah (i.e., Quran):

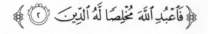

"Whoever does righteous acts while he is believes." [73]

﴾ فَٱعۡبُدِ ٱللَّهَ مُخۡلِصًا لَّهُ ٱلدِّينَ ۝ ﴿

"So worship Allaah making the religion sincerely for Him." [74]

---

[73] Taha[20:112]

﴿ قُلْ إِن كُنتُمْ تُحِبُّونَ ٱللَّهَ فَٱتَّبِعُونِي يُحْبِبْكُمُ ٱللَّهُ ﴾

"Say, if you love Allaah then follow Me Allaah will love you." [75]

These three verses, when they are applied to an action then it is a righteous action. And if it (the action) is void of a verse from the three, then it is an unrighteous deed meaning corrupted.

His statement:

﴿ وَمَن يَعْمَلْ مِنَ ٱلصَّٰلِحَٰتِ وَهُوَ مُؤْمِنٌ ﴾

"And whoever does righteous acts while he is a believer" [76]

Means: a Muslim so a believer here means a Muslim because the deeds of a disbeliever is not accepted, and this is the first condition. Allaah's statement:

﴿ فَٱعْبُدِ ٱللَّهَ مُخْلِصًا لَّهُ ٱلدِّينَ (٢) ﴾

"So worship Allaah making the religion sincerely for Him."

Includes the second condition, which is sincerity. The statement of Allaah:

---

[74] Az-Zumar [39:2]
[75] Ali-Imran [3:31]
[76] Taha [20:112]

﴿ قُلْ إِن كُنتُمْ تُحِبُّونَ اللَّهَ فَاتَّبِعُونِي يُحْبِبْكُمُ اللَّهُ ﴾

"Say, if you love Allaah then follow me, Allaah will love you."

This contains the third condition which is following the Prophet ﷺ – Peace be upon him; and from here, this supplication...

﴿ اهْدِنَا ٱلصِّرَٰطَ ٱلْمُسْتَقِيمَ ٦ ﴾

"Guide us to the straight path."

Is the most inclusive and beneficial supplications period.

Guidance from another aspect is divided in two categories:

1. General Guidance
2. Specific Guidance

As for **General Guidance**: It is in the Quran abundantly like His -the Exalted- statement:

﴿ قَدَّرَ فَهَدَىٰ ٣ ﴾

"He has measured and then guided." 77

---

77 Al-A' la [87:3]

This includes even animals. So He has guided everyone to its guidance. For example if you were to push a cow towards a fire like it is water, it truly would flee from it. This is guidance from Allaah and is called **general guidance**. That includes mankind, the animal kingdom, and all things. As for His statement:

"Verily you do not guide whom you like but Allaah guide whom He wills." [78]

This is for **"specific guidance"** meaning guidance of success granted by Allaah.

And there is a good observation with this statement….

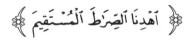

"guide us to the straight path"

If you took Tafseer Ibn Jareer, Ibn Katheer, or Bagawi, and you wanted to know the meaning of *"the straight path"* you would find many statements; however, these statements there are not between them difference that oppose the truth in explanation the Quran or the Sunnah; rather, all of them (i.e., Their statements) are

---

[78] Qasas [28:56]

differences related to diversity, and differences related to contradiction has not been established from them.

The Philosophers, Orientalists, Soofees, and the Blind Followers try to find this differences related to contradiction from the Salaf; however, they return with empty hands and they did not find anything.

So the Salaf there cannot be found from them differing in the Quran or the Sunnah save the differing related to diversity or differing in forms of reciting the Quran. For example:

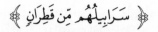

"Their garments will be of pitch" [79]

This word some of the Salaf have explained it saying: *"A pitch is that which camels are coated with."* [80]

And some of them said: *"Copper intensely hot."* [mufradat Quran],   this is because the Arabic word for "pitch" in the verse is **qitiran**. And some scholars say that the word qitiran means copper extremely hot. Like what comes in Surah Kahf [verse:96] and Rahman [verse:44].

---

[79] Ibrahim [14:50]
[80] Noted from Al-Hasan Al-Basri and Jaabir bin Zayd, 'Akramah Maw'la' ibn 'Abbas. Just like what is mentioned in Tafseer At-Tabari (13/ 255-256) and in the book "Ad-Durr Al-Man'thur" (5/ 59).

The rare obscure recital is mentioned for the sake of understanding the correct recital and not to be recited because it is a form of reciting. This is the reason the scholars have written about the "rare obscure recitals" from them is the book *"Al-Muhtasab Fee Al-Qiraa't Ash-Shaith"*.

None of this is called differing that opposes the truth. This one says it is two words **"qitir" (copper)** and **" an" (extremely hot)** that means extremely hot copper and the other one say it's one word and if so then it means pitch or that which coats a camel.

So because of the differing in the recitals the explanations slightly differ. Like this, is the Straight Path. The Straight Path is Islam and the Quran, and it is following the Prophet ﷺ like this all of these statements do not have any conflict.

Islam is the Quran as is the Quran is Islam. Islam is following the Prophet ﷺ, and this is called differing related to diversity that do not oppose the truth.

For this reason, Shaykhul Islam wrote a small independent book on this type of differing in a small excellent treatise called *"Various Permissible Types of Differing"*. Small in size and major in meaning and building a foundation, and it was published some time ago when *"Majmoo'a Fatawa"* was published it was included in it. Likewise was included in it a section for Fiqh, and principles of Fiqh.

I had an individual copy of it before the Majmoo' was published. He said in this treatise similar to what he said in his excellent treatise *"Introduction to Principles of Tafseer"* that I hope you try to benefit from and study this introduction because no one has written on this subject of principles of Tafseer like this introduction. In it are things that are rare to find in any other book. He made a section in it on differing and categorized it into **"Differing related to contradiction"** and **"Differing related to diversity"**.

He mentioned in that same chapter, "that differences related to contradiction was not possible to exist during the time of the Salaf while at the same time, it did exist differing related to diversity; and contradiction are of two categories: Either differing related to contraction or differing related to opposites and this type of differing cause harm.

As for the differing related to diversity, this is knowledge recommended for us to strive for and learn in the religion from our scholars and leaders. That cannot happen unless we study their books nor are we able to understand the narrations without them and their books. And it is obligatory upon you to strive hard for that until they connect you with the Quran and Sunnah.

This is the case with us because we do not possess the tools and means they had with them, so it is an obligation on us to imitate them. In the statement of Allaah:

﴿ صِرَٰطَ ٱلَّذِينَ أَنْعَمْتَ عَلَيْهِمْ غَيْرِ ٱلْمَغْضُوبِ عَلَيْهِمْ وَلَا ٱلضَّآلِّينَ ۝ ﴾

"The path of those you have bestowed upon them your bounty, nor those who have a wrath upon them nor those who are astray".

Here, Allaah mentions types of mankind in his statement,

﴿ صِرَٰطَ ٱلَّذِينَ أَنْعَمْتَ عَلَيْهِمْ ﴾

"The path of those whom you have bestowed upon them your bounty".

They are those whom Allaah clarified whom they are in Surah Nisaa,

﴿ مِّنَ ٱلنَّبِيِّــۧنَ وَٱلصِّدِّيقِينَ وَٱلشُّهَدَآءِ وَٱلصَّٰلِحِينَ ﴾

"From all the prophets, extremely truthful, martyrs, and the righteous" [81]

---

[81] Nisaa [4:69]

That means the scholars who are workers for the religion they are the first group (or type of people).

The second type...

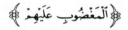

"wrath upon them"

Are the scholars who do not practice their knowledge. This is the reason Allaah has mentioned His anger and wrath upon cursed Jews because they disobey knowledge:

﴿ يَعْرِفُونَهُ كَمَا يَعْرِفُونَ أَبْنَاءَهُمْ ﴾

"They know it (the religion) like they know their children" 82

Third type: are those who are astray they are the ignorant. The Prophet ﷺ had explained these last two categories or types when He was asked who are those who have a wrath upon them and those who are astray? He said:

هُمُ الْيَهُودُ وَ النَّصَارَى

"They are the Jews and the Christians". 83

---

82 Al-Baqarah [2:146]

The Jews are the example of those with a wrath upon them. The Christians are the example of those who are astray and ignorant.

We benefit from this that everyone who implements the Quran and prophetic traditions then he is from the students of the scholars who practice the knowledge and everyone who learns the Book and Sunnah and yet does not practice it then he is from the students of the Jews and who turns away from the Quran and Sunnah are the students of Christians, the meaning of all of this is that he is like them.

Either he resembles the righteous or the non-righteous, and they are with the categories of those who have a wrath on them and those who are astray. Then in this Surah were mentioned some of its previous benefits that Allaah began with Tawheed first which shows that the first obligation is Tawheed. This Tawheed where do we get it from? We get it from the Quran.

This is because if it was from the intellect or by investigating just like the philosophers and orientalists do and the people of rhetoric truly Allaah would have mentioned it to us and He would not have revealed to us a complete Surah including Tawheed.

---

83 Imam Ahmad collected it in his Musnad (4/378) and At-Tirmidhi collected it in his "Jaamee'" (hadeeth 2954) from the hadeeth of 'Adee bin Haatim, may Allaah be pleased with him.

Just as He began His Book to teach us Tawheed, likewise He sealed His Book with Tawheed to teach us.

Meaning, Allaah the Exalted is saying to us: *"Just as I command you that the first obligation upon you to learn is Tawheed, also the last obligation upon you is to die upon Tawheed."*

Allaah says,

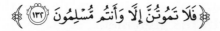

"Do not die except while you are submitting."[84]

Meaning: *"Except while you are single out Allaah alone for worship."* Just as you are the people of Tawheed in the beginning of your lives, you must also be from the people of Tawheed in the end of your life.

Like this, is how the Quran ties the first of it to the last of it. Allaah begins it with Tawheed with these types of indications so now we want to link between Tawheed in the beginning of Suratul-Fatihah with the Tawheed that is at the beginning of An-Naas. We say Allaah says,

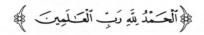

---

[84] Al-Baqarah [2:132]

"All praise is due to Allaah the lord of all that exists"

And He says,

﴿ قُلْ أَعُوذُ بِرَبِّ ٱلنَّاسِ ۝ ﴾

"Say we seek refuge with the lord of mankind"

So the lord of all that exists is the lord of mankind. In His statement,

﴿ ٱلرَّحْمَٰنِ ٱلرَّحِيمِ ۝ مَٰلِكِ يَوْمِ ٱلدِّينِ ﴾

"The most merciful the most compassionate. The king of the day of reckoning"

And in His statement,

﴿ مَلِكِ ٱلنَّاسِ ۝ ﴾

"King of mankind"

This is Tawheed in Allaah's names and attributes. In His statements,

﴿ إِيَّاكَ نَعْبُدُ وَإِيَّاكَ نَسْتَعِينُ ۝ ﴾

"You alone we worship and seek assistance"

And...

$$\{ \text{إِلَٰهِ ٱلنَّاسِ} (٣) \}$$

"The god of mankind".

Therefore, Suratul-Fatihah contains Tawheed completely in the beginning of the Quran just as Surah An-Naas contains complete Tawheed at the end of the Quran. These two subtle two points:

1). The first obligation is Tawheed,

2). The second obligation is to die on Tawheed, just as Allaah says,

$$\{ \text{فَلَا تَمُوتُنَّ إِلَّا وَأَنتُم مُّسْلِمُونَ} (١٣٢) \}$$

"Do not die except while you are submitting"
85

It is obligatory on you to be concerned with Tawheed in the beginning and ending of your life. This is what the scholars of eloquence call *"returning the back to the front"* and this is an Arabic way of speaking mentioned in the Arabic science of *'Ilmul-Badee.*

---

85 Al-Baqarah [2: 132]

Meaning: That you end your speech with the likes of what you begin with. This way of speaking the Arabs love it as a way of speaking, and the Quran was revealed in a clear Arab tongue.

For this reason, The Quran addresses the Arabs with what they understand and know, and it never addresses them with that which they do not know. With this you can use as a proof against that which some people say who are negligent in their religion, specifically those groups upon philosophy, rhetoric, and false speech that there is in the Quran that which the scholars do not know the meaning of. This statement is at the highest level of corruption and impossible to exist in the Quran that which the scholars do not know the meaning of.

This is because among the scholars are Arabs and the Quran was revealed in a clear Arab tongue. So how could the Arabs be ignorant of the meaning of the Quran while it is in their language?

However, what is possible is that a person can be ignorant of something whether he is Arab or non-Arab that is in the Quran in specific matters just as Ibn Abbaas –May Allaah be pleased with him - pointed towards in his statement *"The Tafseer is based upon four ways:*

 1.-**Explanation** that no one has an excuse of being ignorant about.

2.-**Explanation** no one knows it save the scholars.

3.-**Explanation** no one knows it save the Arabs

4.-**Explanation** no one knows it save Allaah (At-Tabari in the intro of his tafseer)

As for the one who has no excuse for being ignorant about it like...

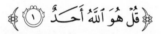

"Say, He Allaah is unique". [86]

No one has an excuse for being ignorant of its meaning because included in it are clear words that do not need reflection, or deep study.

The explanation no one knows except the scholars like the unrestricted and restricted parts of the Quran, the general and detailed aspects of the Quran, the abrogated and abrogating parts of the Quran, and the specific parts of it. These are the abstracted sciences that the scholars specialize in not the common folk. For example, Allaah said:

---

[86] Al-Ikhlaas [112:1]

﴿ وَٱلْمُطَلَّقَٰتُ يَتَرَبَّصْنَ بِأَنفُسِهِنَّ ثَلَٰثَةَ قُرُوٓءٖ ﴾

"The divorced women waiting period within themselves is for their menses" [87]

This verse perhaps a common person can comprehend it, but it being specific or restricted, this stops at the scholars and not the common folk.

As for the one who does not know the explanation except the Arab. Like the vocabulary of the Quran as in the Statement of Allaah;

﴿ كَأَنَّهُمْ حُمُرٞ مُّسْتَنفِرَةٞ ۝ فَرَّتْ مِن قَسْوَرَةِۭ ۝ ﴾

"As if they are like fleeing donkeys. Fleeing from a lion." [88]

Both of the verses are from the seven forms of recital and the word; "*qaswara*" is from the strange wording of the Quran that only the Arabs know what it means.

The true Arabs today; they are, '*Kitaabul Ayn*' by Khalil, '*At-tah-heeb*' by Al-Ajhari, '*Al-Maqa-yees* 'by Ibn Larras, '*At-U'bad*' by; As Sagani, '*Lisanul Arab* By; Ibn Manthoor, '*A-Misbaah*' By

---

[87] Al-Baqarah [2-228]
[88] Mudaaththir [74:50-51]

Fayyoorri, and *'Al-Qaamoos'* By Frayroz Abadiyah.

The Arabs that exist today their language has changed because of mingling with non-Arabs. Truly this language is preserved in the books of the scholars - belongs to Allaah the praise and bounty-until the point the evidence has been established upon us, and if it was not preserved in the books how else would we understand the Book of our Lord and the Traditions of our Prophet – peace be upon him?

So Allaah has established the arguments against us by decreeing that there be sincere men who strove hard and preserved this language from every aspect of it. Whether that be grammar, morphology, vocabulary, eloquence, or the principles of the language all of this has been recorded.

The last aspects of Tafseer is that which no one knows but Allaah and that is the essence of how Allaah attributes are; no one knows their true reality except Allaah and likewise the minute details of what's going to occur on the Day of Reckoning, Chastisement, Paradise, and Hell from those affairs we have not been told about in detail no one knows about them save Allaah.

So was presented earlier that the explanation of the Quran is in four aspects. Now looking at that from another angle or direction the explanation of the Quran can be known by four other aspects:

-**Explanation** of the Quran by Quran.

-**Explanation** of the Quran by the prophetic Sunnah

-**Explanation** of the Quran by the statements of the companions and the followers

-**Explanation** of the Quran by the Arabic Language.

CLOSING WORDS

In summary, we are able to say Surah Fatihah comprises of six things, and they are the following:

-Tawheed by its three categories

-The positions of the people in regard to this Tawheed and they are three positions

The Tawheed that Allaah clarified at the beginning of the Surah is Unity of Allaah in His Lordship, which is Unity of Allaah in His actions like creating, providing, causing life and death.

He mentioned unity of Allaah in His names and attributes and the details of that were presented. He mentioned Unity in Allaah's worship and that singling out Allaah alone in the actions of His servants like prayer, and almsgiving.

As for the positions of people from Tawheed He (Allaah) presented the first position in His statement:

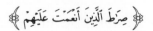

"The path of those whom you have bestowed you bounty upon them."

So Who are they?

Answer: They are those whom Allaah bestowed: The Prophets, extremely truthful, Martyrs, and the Righteous; They learned Tawheed and implemented it.

Then He followed that with the position of the Jews and the likes of them, and they are the cursed hated Jews who learned knowledge but did not practice it. That is understood in His statement:

"Not those who have a wrath upon them".

Next He followed that up with the position of the Christians and their likes from the superstitions in their belief. That is in His statement,

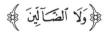

"Nor those who are astray"

And their position is them lacking learning Tawheed, not to mention acting upon it.

These are the general levels of mankind with regards to Tawheed and its Three Categories.

The point is this Noble Surah is tremendous. Therefore, it is called:

-**The Seven Most Recited Verses** because it is seven verses and because it is repeated in each unit of prayer.

-**and The Magnificent Quran** because it is inclusive to the message of the whole Quran.

So it (Surah Fatihah) truly consist of six things:

✓ The Three Categories of Tawheed

✓ And the three levels of mankind with regards to Tawheed.

This is what was in my capabilities to present in regards to the explanation of this tremendous Surah that which if time allowed for its explanation we would benefit from it many things that the scholars said about it.

We ask Allaah, The Magnificent, Lord of the Tremendous Throne that He makes us and you guides who are guided. And that He makes us of those who listen to the statements of truth and follow it in the most excellent manner.

Allaah knows best. Forgiveness and peace be upon our Prophet Muhammad, his family, and his companions.

৪৩ ❋ ❋ ❋ ৫৪

NOTES